THROUGH THE LENS OF
THE 3rd EYE!

A NEW PERSPECTIVE!

VISION BEYOND SIGHT!

Eileen McCourt

Through the Lens of the 3rd Eye!

By Eileen McCourt

CONTENTS

About the Author

Eileen McCourt is a retired school teacher of English and History with a Master's degree in History from University College Dublin.

She is also a Reiki Grand Master teacher and practitioner, having qualified in Ireland, England and Spain, and has introduced many of the newer modalities of Reiki healing energy into Ireland for the first time, from Spain and England. Eileen has qualified in England through the Lynda Bourne School of Enlightenment, and in Spain through the Spanish Federation of Reiki with Alessandra Rossin, Bienstar, Santa Eulalia, Ibiza.

Regular workshops and courses are held in Elysium Wellness, Newry, County Down; New Moon Holistics N.I. Carrickfergus, County Antrim; Angel Times Limerick; Holistic Harmony Omagh, County Tyrone; Celtic School of Sound Healing, Swords, County Dublin; Reiki Healing Bettystown, County Meath and Moonbeams, Carrigaline County Cork, where Eileen has been teaching the following to both practitioner and teacher levels:

- **Tibetan Usui Reiki levels 1, 2, 3 (Inner Master) 4 (teacher) and Grand Master**

- Okuna Reiki (Atlantean and Lemurian)

- Karuna- Prakriti (Tibetan Usui and Hindu)

- Rahanni Celestial Healing

- Fire Spirit Reiki (Christ Consciousness and Holy Spirit)

- Mother Mary Reiki

- Mary Magdalene Reiki

- Archangels Reiki

- Archangels Ascended Masters Reiki

- Reiki Seraphim

- Violet Flame Reiki

- Lemurian Crystal Reiki

- Golden Eagle Reiki (Native North American Indian)

- Golden Chalice Reiki

- Golden Rainbow Ray Reiki

- Goddesses of Light Reiki

- Unicorn Reiki

- **Pegasus Reiki**

- **Elementals Reiki**

- **Dragon Reiki**

- **Dolphin Reiki**

- **Pyramid of Goddess Isis Reiki**

- **Kundalini Reiki**

- **Psychic Energy Surgery Healing**

Details of all of these modalities can be found on Eileen's website, together with dates and venues of courses and workshops.

This is Eileen's **48th** book.

Previous publications include:

- *'Living the Magic'*, published in December 2014

- *'This Great Awakening'*, September 2015

- *'Spirit Calling! Are You Listening?'*, January 2016

- *'Working With Spirit: A World of Healing'*, January 2016

- *'Life's But A Game! Go With The Flow!',* March 2016

- *'Rainbows, Angels and Unicorns!',* April 2016

- *'........And That's The Gospel Truth!',* September 2016

- *'The Almost Immaculate Deception! The Greatest Scam in History?',* September 2016

- *'Are Ye Not Gods?' The true inner meanings of Jesus' teachings and messages',* March 2017

- *'Jesus Lost and Found',* July 2017

- *'Behind Every Great Man........ Mary Magdalene Twin Flame of Jesus',* July 2017

- *'Out of the Mind and into the Heart: Our Spiritual Journey with Mary Magdalene',* August 2017

- *'Divinely Designed: The Oneness of the Totality of ALL THAT IS',* January 2018. Also in *Audiobook*, May 2019

- *'Resurrection or Resuscitation? What really happened in That Tomb?',* May 2018

- *'Music of the Spheres: Connecting to the Great*

Universal Consciousness and to ALL THAT IS through the music of Irish composer /pianist Pat McCourt', June 2018

- **'Chakras, Crystals, Colours and Drew the Dragon: A child's second Spiritual book',** July 2018

- *'The Voice of a Master: It is Jesus Himself Who Speaks: Know Thyself',* December 2018

- *'Kundalini',* January 2019

- *'Brave Little Star Child Comes To Earth'* - Audiobook- April 2019

- *'The Truth will set you free. - Christianity: Where did it all begin?'* May 2019

- '*Titus Flavius Josephus: Did Josephus write the gospels?'* June 2019

- *'Homo SPACIENS: We Are Not From Planet Earth! Our connection with UFOs, ETs and Ancient Civilisations'* August 2019

- *'Those Strange Looking Men In Their Flying Machines: Visitors From Beyond Time and Space? Or From Planet Earth? - ETs, UFOs and Who Knows What'* September 2019

- *'I Want to Break Free: Helping our Planet Earth*

ascend to a higher vibration of Love, Joy, Peace and Happiness for all. We can do it!' November 2019

- *'The Universe is Mental! Understanding the 7 Spiritual Laws of the Universe, the Hermetic Principles that govern Creation'* January 2020

- *'To Be Or Not To Be.... The Man of Stratford who was never to be Shakespeare: Exposing the deception that was William Shakespeare'* February 2020

- *'If Not Shakespeare, Then Who? Unmasking the Real Bard of Avon! '* April 2020

- *'What On Earth Is Happening? 2020: Year of Balance: Rise of the Divine Feminine'* April 2020

- *'Creating a New World! - Nature WILL be obeyed! - The greatest lesson never taught, but which we need to learn'* May 2020

- *'Humanity's Greatest Challenge? Breaking out of the vortex of ignorance and superstition'* May 2020

- *'Puppets on a String! But! The Strings have been broken! We are free!'* July 2020

embedded in myths and legends of our sacred sites' . - November 2022

- *'Ancient Ancestors Calling! With words of wisdom and knowledge for today's world'.* - December 2022

- *Wake Up! This is it! The Great Apocalypse! - There is nothing hidden that will not be revealed'.* - May 2023

- *'The Simulator. Are we living in a simulation? Are we trapped? If so, how do we escape?'* - July 2023

- *'The Soul Net! Does it exist? Are we a trawling ground for energy vampires and other-worldly parasites? How do we avoid getting caught?'* - September 2023

- *'This is OUR STORY! - The story of Humanity! - As in the ancient Sumerian Clay Tablets! - And the Missing Link?'* - January 2024

And now this current book: *'Through The Lens of the 3rd Eye. A new perspective! Vision beyond sight!'*

Podcasts for each of these 48 books can be viewed on Eileen's website and on her author page.

Eileen has also just recently re-published a series of 5 local history books under the title '*Finding Our Way Back*'. These were first published in the 1980s:

Book One: '*Strange Happenings*' - a 1988 collection of local ghost stories and local cures and charms, collected by the students of Saint Patrick's College Armagh.

Book Two: '*Tell Me More, Grandad!*' - a collection of school day memories collected from grandparents and great-grandparents in 1990.

Book Three: '*Gather In, Gather In*', - a collection of children's games and rhymes, 1942-1943, by the late Mr. Paddy Hamill, collected from the pupils in Lislea No 2 Primary School 1939 to 1947 when Mr. Hamill was Principal

Book Four: '*A Peep Into The Past: Armagh in Great-Granny's day*' - Earlier maps of Armagh, explaining how Armagh got its street names, together with photographs of streets and shop-fronts in the early 20th century. Also included is information on schools and education in Armagh in the 19th Century; newspaper articles of interest from 1848; traders in Armagh in 1863 and markets and fairs in Armagh, - of which there were many!

Book Five: "*The Poor Law And The Workhouse In Armagh 1838-1948*' - prepared when Eileen was on secondment in the Public Record Office of Northern Ireland, 1980-1981, under the scholarship scheme provided for teachers by the Department of Education. The resulting publication was used in local schools for coursework for examination purposes. Primary sources include the Armagh workhouse registers and minute books, which are all held in the Northern Ireland Public Record Office in Belfast; government commissions and reports; annual reports of the Poor Law Commission for Ireland 1847-1921, and photographs of the inside and outside of Armagh workhouse, now part of Tower Hill Hospital, taken in 1989 by the late Mary Donnelly (nee Finn), Saint Patrick's College, Armagh.

The recent series of FB weekly videos, '*Our Great Awakening',* together with the previous series '*The Nature of........*' with Eileen and Declan Quigley, Shamanic practitioner and teacher can also be viewed on Eileen's website and on YouTube, together with a series of healing meditations and Shamanic journeys.

Recent Full Moon Meditations with Declan Quigley, Jennifer Maddy and Brenda Murnaghan can be viewed on Eileen's YouTube channel, - access through website.

Eileen has also recorded 6 guided meditation CDs with her brother, composer/pianist Pat McCourt:

- *'Celestial Healing'*

- *'Celestial Presence'*

- *'Cleansing, energising and balancing the Chakras'*

- *'Ethereal Spirit' - Meditation on the 'I Am Presence'*

- *'Open the Door to Archangel Michael'*

- *'Healing with Archangel Raphael'*

Eileen's first DVD, *'Living the Magic'* features a live interview in which Eileen talks about matters Spiritual.

All publications are available from Amazon online and all publications and CDs are in Angel and Holistic centres around the country, as specified on website.

Please visit also the BLOG page on Eileen's website.

Website: www.celestialhealing8.co.uk

Author page: www.tinyurl.com/EileenMcCourt

YouTube channel:

https://www.youtube.com/channel/UChJPprUDnl9Eeu
0IrRjGsqw

ACKNOWLEDGEMENTS

Book number *48!*

Thank you *yet again* to my publishers Dr. Steve Green and Don Hale OBE, for all their work and support, and without whom none of these books would ever actually materialise!

And of course, not forgetting all of you who are buying my books and CDs wherever in the world you are, and all who have taken the time to give me feed-back, and to write reviews for me, both in my books and on Amazon. You are greatly appreciated!

Thank you to all who attend my courses, workshops and meditation sessions, sharing your amazing energies, taking us on such wonderful journeys and through such amazing experiences! We are all so blessed!

Thank you to all of you who are, and have been facilitating my workshops, courses, visits to ancient sacred sites, Facebook videos, etc. and to those of you involved in all the reprographics work, - which never seems to end!

And thank you to all of you who have been following

me on Facebook. I sincerely hope the posts are bringing some comfort and help to you in these present rapidly changing times when so many people are paralyzed with fear, anxiety and uncertainty.

But all is well! All is as it should be! The Earth and all in her and on her are moving into a higher energy vibration level - all are ascending! So hold on! Don't give up! Not now! Not now when we have already come so far!

And as always, I give thanks for all the great blessings that are constantly being sent our way in this wonderful, loving, abundant universe.

Namaste!

1st February 2024

FOREWORD

The 3rd Eye is not called the 3rd **EYE** for nothing!

This watchful, sentient doorway to higher levels of consciousness, providing vision beyond our limited physical sight, the 3rd Eye unfortunately continues to remain dormant, mystical and mysterious to many, - an untapped, unplumbed, unmitigated source of the highest-voltage energy.

We are all here on this earth dimension to grow in consciousness and awareness, for individual soul expansion and for the collective spiritual growth of all humanity. **Growth!** - That's what we are all about! And the key to growth? Growth has nothing to do with the number of earth years we manage to clock up. Rather, as in the words of Lao Tzu, the semi-legendary sixth century BCE Chinese philosopher, credited with founding the philosophical system of Taoism:

'The key to growth is the introduction of higher dimensions of consciousness into our awareness.'

And how do we introduce and attain higher dimensions of consciousness into our awareness and into our process of spiritual growth? - **Through our 3rd Eye!** That's how pivotal and central our 3rd Eye is in our life!

So what exactly is our 3rd Eye? How does it work? Why do we need to activate it? How do we actually activate it? What happens when the 3rd Eye is activated? And what exactly are the benefits from having our 3rd Eye activated?

That's what this book is all about!

The 3rd Eye is by no means a new discovery! Yes, it may well be relatively new to Western culture, which tends to follow the scientific path, where if you cannot experience something with one or other of your five physical senses, - if you cannot see, hear, smell, taste or feel it, - then it does not exist. But numerous spiritual belief systems across the world have been practising 3rd Eye awakening for centuries, - Buddhism, Hinduism, Taoism, for example, as well as ancient civilisations such as ancient Egypt and the Mayan and Indian civilisations. It may indeed seem strange that the Western scientific world has never embraced this spiritual concept of the 3rd Eye, simply because it is a sentient, unseen energy force, - while at the same time accepting gravity as an unseen energy force holding us all together in the universe, and electricity as an unseen energy force which is so vital to our world today.

But in just the same way as unseen gravity and

electricity can be harnessed, so too the unseen energy of the human chakra system can also be harnessed, to regulate many of our physical and mental functions, and bring us physical and spiritual health, nourishment and well-being. And the 3rd Eye is the 6th chakra in the human body energy field, right in the middle of the forehead, aligned vertically along the spine with all the other chakras, both front and back of the body.

We are spiritual beings and not just physical beings. But we have been programmed and conditioned from we are born into this earth-plane dimension to feed our physical needs and desires, and to see our existence here simply as a materialistic one. We have been denied knowledge of our greater cosmic connection, higher levels of consciousness and other-level energy dimensional realities, drip-fed a restrictive and limiting diet by controlling religions, and led to believe in a punishing, vengeful God, out to get us if we do not obey '*His*' rules. Sin, punishment, condemnation, - a continuing ongoing cycle of an agenda deliberately instigated to keep certain factions of society in power and control. We have indeed been programmed and conditioned to adhere to someone else's agenda!

Sci-fi has now become fact in our world. And this fiction-turned-fact includes computer programmes and games! What was, a very short time ago, simply fantasy and fun games, has become our real world, as these computer games are now being played out for real. War, aggression, violence is now being played out for real on our world stage! And what we see with our physical eyes, - we take this all as our reality. But it is all just a game! And we see this game being played out in front of us through our limited two physical eyes.

But! Through the lens of our **3rd Eye** we get a very different picture! A very different perspective! We get vision beyond sight! We get the real story, the truth, - which our limited physical vision cannot see.

The problems in our world are neither economic nor political. Our problem is a spiritual problem. And a spiritual problem needs a spiritual solution, not an economic or political solution.

And we can only find that spiritual solution to our world problems when we look **through the lens of our 3rd Eye.** When we have **vision beyond sight!**

So let us look!

Chapter 1:

What is the 3rd Eye?

From an esoteric or spiritual point of view, the 3rd Eye is the mystical *'inner eye'*, the *'eye of the Soul'*, the *'all-seeing eye'* that is able to see reality, which is not what appears to our two very limited physical eyes, but the more *'subtle'* one, seeing beyond the gateway of consciousness. This 3rd Eye is able to *'see'* the invisible, to *'see'* beyond ordinary vision, to *'perceive'* the 95% of reality that our human eyes do not perceive, - our perception with our ordinary senses is severely limited to only about 5% of what actually exists out there. So it is our 3rd Eye that allows us to *'see'* the totality of All That Is. - Vision beyond sight!

Considered the gateway to the inner realms of consciousness, psychic visions and clairvoyance, the 3rd Eye is a trainable chakra that can allow individuals to tap into cognitive functions that can supersede ordinary logic. But not everyone gets the opportunity to open their 3rd Eye simply because the awareness of its power still remains unknown to many people. But when activated, it opens the door to a new world of spiritual possibilities.

Often called '*seers*', individuals with an actively open 3rd Eye chakra have access to a list of skills that help make navigating life, relationships, and emotions far less problematic and taxing. An open 3rd Eye can also improve our perception of the spiritual realms that exist all around us, and run parallel to our own physical world reality.

This 3rd Eye, in the ancient Hindu and Buddhist tradition, corresponds with the sixth chakra, the Ajna, located at the centre of the forehead between the eyebrows. In these traditions, this centre represents the '*inner eye'*, able to perceive reality beyond the ordinary vision. It is the door of clairvoyance, of superior vision, new perspectives, increasing awareness, higher levels of consciousness, and spiritual enlightenment. The 3rd Eye is the connection with one's intuitive mind, with the Higher Self, let us also say with one's Soul.

The 3rd Eye is the centre of intuition, intellect, personal magnetism and light. This is where creativity and inspiration combine, and psychic abilities and gifts are also focused. When the 3rd Eye Chakra is healthy and balanced, it helps remove negative and self-centred attitudes, and facilitates intuition and wisdom. As the seat of inner knowing and intuition, the 3rd Eye is associated with '*light*', and in spiritual terms, light stands for true understanding, clarity and '*insight*'. We all know the phrase to '*throw light on something*'. And if we draw a line connecting our two physical eyes with our 3rd Eye, what shape do we get? We get a triangle! A triangle that is said to represent Enlightenment! Enlightenment meaning vision, - inner vision! Vision beyond physical sight! Vision beyond and within!

Our 3rd Eye enables us to look clearly not only in the past or future, but also across dimensions. It is the prominent seat of intuition and awareness, acting as a control centre for many physical, emotional and spiritual practices.

Our two '*physical*' eyes are used to perceive the material world, while our 3rd Eye helps us see the world beyond this material plane. A world of multiple dimensions! Picture the Cosmic Hologram! Multiple realities and dimensions, all connected and inter-relating! All microcosms contained within the one all-enveloping macrocosm! And it is our 3rd Eye that enables psychics and mediums to travel through these multiple dimensions of reality. And travelling through these multiple levels of reality, - this is how and when they '*see*' beyond this physical earth dimension. And all through the lens of the 3rd Eye!

The 3rd Eye is associated with the colour indigo, - all colours being a vibration of energy. And why indigo? Simply because indigo is considered a deeply spiritual colour in numerous traditions across the world. In general it is seen as a colour that can boost our awareness of ourselves and the world around us, helping us to see things as they are and not as we would like them to be. It is also associated with wisdom, intuition and higher consciousness levels, and so it can be used to raise our consciousness and access other states of being that are not usually available to us. This is also why the colour indigo is usually associated with the practice of meditation.

And of course, we are familiar with the spiritual Violet Flame Energy! The Violet Flame Energy of transmutation! The Violet Flame Energy of protection!

Indigo is also seen as a colour of balance between the fiery energy of red and the calming energy of blue. So it represents vitality and dynamism, but also tranquility. And without tranquility it is impossible to become aware of our true nature. And indigo is also related to transitions - both from life to death and from one place of existence to another. This is important because, as already mentioned, an aligned 3rd Eye chakra helps us perceive things that are beyond this earthly plane of reality.

So, in all ancient spiritual belief systems, the 3rd Eye is associated with wisdom, intuition, self-reflection, logic and inner vision.

Third Eye in Hinduism: The word '*ajna*' comes from Sanskrit, which stands for '*perceiving',* or '*command*' and also means '*beyond wisdom'*. In Hindu customs, a '*tika*' or '*tilak*' - a small, usually red mark, - is placed on the forehead where the 3rd Eye is believed to be. When the 3rd Eye chakra is gently pressed and covered by '*tilak*', the energy of this 3rd Eye chakra is believed to be increased and preserved. The 3rd Eye makes us see inside ourselves - and remember! Whatever we are looking for is already within us.

Third Eye in Buddhism: According to Buddhist beliefs the 3rd Eye is the key to raising our level of consciousness. And when we raise our consciousness level, we see beyond the physical plane and see reality more through the '*eye of the soul'.* This is the '*wisdom eye'* in Buddhist beliefs, - wisdom, discipline and meditation being the three main teachings of Buddha.

5

Wisdom can only be gained by seeing the *'right view'*. And the *'right view',* the ultimate truth, - as opposed to the relative truth which we see with our two physical eyes, - can only be seen through the lens of the 3rd Eye.

Third Eye in Taoism: In Taoism, the flow of life force energy through the entire body is controlled through the 3rd Eye Chakra, with mindfulness and meditation centred on the 3rd Eye leading to inner vitality and increased spiritual awareness.

Third Eye in Egyptian Mythology: In Egyptian mythology, the 3rd Eye, also known as the *'Eye of Horus',* the *'Udjat eye'* or the *'All-seeing eye'* is a symbol that represents well-being, healing and protection. It derives from the mythical conflict between the Egyptian god Horus, son of the Goddess Isis, with his rival Set, in which Set tore out or destroyed one or both of Horus's eyes and the eye was subsequently healed or returned to Horus with the assistance of another deity, such as Thoth. Horus subsequently offered the eye to his deceased father Osiris, and its revitalising power sustained Osiris in the afterlife. The Eye of Horus was thus equated with funerary offerings, as well as with all the offerings given to deities in temple ritual. It could also represent other concepts, such as the moon, whose waxing and waning was likened to the injury and restoration of the eye.

The Eye of Horus is seen as responsible for the expansion of our perceptive qualities. The ancient Egyptian god Horus was a sky deity, and many Egyptian texts say that Horus's right eye was the sun and his left eye the moon. He is most often depicted with a falcon's head and is crowned with the pschent, the emblem of the pharaohs of Egypt. So the eye of Horus is considered a magical and divine relic that allows its owner to see beyond the visible, and into the future.

And today, the eye of Horus is still worn, in the form of jewellery for example, so that its holder benefits from its supposed powers of protection. Moreover, nowadays, this eye is found on the hulls of Egyptian fishing boats to ensure that sailors can travel peacefully under the '*divine protection*' of the falcon-headed god.

So, as we have just seen, the 3rd Eye is associated with our sixth chakra. And each of our chakras in turn is associated with a particular and specific gland in our body. While the chakras are invisible centres of energy, their corresponding organs and glands are physical and tangible. And so problems with a particular gland can cause blockages in the corresponding chakra.

And the 3rd Eye Chakra? With which particular gland is the 3rd Eye chakra associated? - The *pineal* gland!

The pineal gland belongs to the endocrine system of the human body, which is the system of hormone-producing glands necessary for various bodily functions.

Let us now look at this pineal gland!

Chapter 2:

The pineal gland

We are spiritual beings having a physical experience. We are all in a physical body here on this third dimension earth energy vibration level, our body being the organic vessel through which our consciousness experiences our physical reality. So as both spiritual and physical beings, our brain connects to higher states of energy and consciousness, as well as to all that is around us on this more dense third dimension energy vibration level.

There must, therefore, be some sort of a connecting point somewhere within our being, that enables us to connect with the higher energy forces, the higher levels of consciousness, while still remaining in our physical body.

And yes, there is! And it is called the '*pineal gland*'!

The enigma, the mystery that is the pineal gland! The subject of controversy through the ages! The source of the mystical dimension of our life! Working in many mystical ways and holding many mysteries! - It is the many mystical sides of this gland that make it interesting to know more about it.

And it is this same spot that is also referred to as the chakra known as the *'Third Eye'*. Since ancient times yogis have always given much importance to this spot between the two eyebrows. This is the place where they believe the soul resides.

The legendary Indian sage, Sage Vyas, taught that there is an invisible hole in this region between the two eyebrows, which is luminous and spreads light. It spreads coronal light and by focusing on this light, he said he could see beings between earth and the higher spaces, so it is believed that this gland connects the person to the higher world.

Maharsi Patanjali, also a legendary Indian sage, in the third chapter of *'Yogi Sutra'*, says that while focusing on this coronal light, we can have a vision of *'siddhas'*, hence some practitioners of yoga say that while meditating at this area, they can see bright light, and they just enjoy being in that state. The word *'Siddha'* is Sanskrit and means *'perfected one'* and is a term that is used widely in Indian religions and culture. It also means *'one who is accomplished'*, and refers to perfected masters who have achieved a high degree of perfection of the intellect as well as liberation or enlightenment. In Jainism, the term is used to refer to the liberated souls. Siddha may also refer to one who has attained a '*siddhi*', - meaning paranormal capabilities.

So knowledge of this pineal gland and its association with the so-called '*third eye*', also known as the '*all-seeing eye*', dates back to very ancient times and we can find so many representations in various cultures throughout human history. In fact this symbol of the '*all-seeing eye*' is everywhere! Even on the US dollar bill! And in numerous sacred temples around the world, - such as the Cai Dai Temple in Vietnam, where the altar in the prayer hall is known as the '*Altar of the Eye*', - the '*All-seeing Eye*'.

The 17th century philosopher and scientist René Descartes in both his first book '*Treatise of Man*', and in his last book, '*The Passions of the Soul*' described the pineal gland as being '*the principal seat of the soul and the place in which all our thoughts are formed.*' In his '*Treatise of Man*', he describes humans as creatures created by God, and having two ingredients, - a body and a soul. In the '*Passions of the Soul*', he emphasised that the soul is joined to the whole body by '*a certain very small gland situated in the middle of the brain's substance and suspended above the passage through which the spirits in the brain's anterior cavities communicate with those in its posterior cavities.'* Descartes gave importance to this particular structure as it was the only unpaired component of the brain. Today, it is still referred to as being the Seat of the Soul or the Seat of Consciousness.

Pythagoras, Plato, Iamblichus and others wrote of this pineal gland with great reverence. So we must surely want to ask why is the pineal gland represented so clearly in so many different places and cultures throughout history? What is its significance? What is its function? - Elusive and unique it certainly is!

Our brain and DNA are like computer terminals, receiving and transmitting data and information. The brain has two hemispheres, - the right and the left. The pineal gland is a pea-sized organ which is situated between these two hemispheres. It stops growing somewhere between one and two years of age, but from puberty onwards, it begins to increase slightly in weight.

And here is where it all gets **very interesting! Very interesting indeed** when we consider the shape of the pineal gland. Because what shape is the pineal gland? -

It's pine-shaped! And what is so interesting about the pine shape?

The name comes from the Latin *'pinea'* meaning *'pine cone'*. We find references to the pineal gland in numerous ancient cultures in the form of a pine cone, - the ancient Sumerians were the first to give the pineal gland the description of a pine cone. And we can see it in all the symbolism-encoded ancient art. Pinecones were associated with spiritual enlightenment by ancient Babylonians, Egyptians and Greeks. They represent the mysteries between the physical and spiritual worlds, the human brain and the pineal gland. Knowledge of sacred geometry focuses on the pineal gland. The pine cone staff is a symbol of the solar god Osiris and originated in Egypt where he was their messiah who died for his people and whose mother, Isis, was worshipped as the Egyptian version of the later Christian Virgin Mary. The Vatican has the world's largest pine cone that once decorated a fountain in ancient Rome next to a vast temple of Isis. The pope carries a pine cone mounted on his staff, where it symbolises rebirth and the sun. The pine is also the common symbol on images of Hindu gods in India and the Roman-Greek gods. The image of the solar god Osiris in the Egyptian museum in Turino in Italy, carries a pine cone.

So the pine-shaped pineal gland carries a massive amount of symbolism!

But apart from all its symbolism, what is its function?

The pineal gland is responsible for our DNA system. It is capable of making a compound called dimethyltryptamine - DMT for short. This is the same DMT that is found naturally in many types of plants and has psychedelic properties. It is known to cause psychic visions and heightened and vivid perceptions.

Serotonin is a feel-good hormone produced by the pineal gland in the form of melatonin, and is secreted depending on the amount of darkness our eyes receive. Serotonin is a neurotransmitter used in the regulation of body temperature, sense of hunger, satiety and mood. In fact, it is also nicknamed *'the hormone of happiness'*.

The pineal gland actually contains retina cells, pigment similar to that found in the two physical eyes and, just like a physical eye, directly responds to light. But it is also believed to contain light receptors that are thought to be responsible for inner sight or insight.

In other words, apart from our eye cells, even pineal gland cells are light-sensitive, hence the pineal gland is known to regulate our biological clock, since it can sense light and darkness and at night when you close your eyes, everything is dark and in that state, the pineal gland releases melatonin, which is a structurally simple hormone, and this hormone regulates our biological clock as it communicates information about environmental lighting to various parts of the body.

So, when we are asleep at night, our body produces melatonin. Conversely, during the daylight hours, this production of melatonin decreases, and so we are alert and active. Our sleep-wake pattern over the course of a 24-hour day is known as our circadian rhythm, - a natural biological rhythm in the body. It helps control our daily schedule for sleep and wakefulness. Most living things have one. Circadian rhythm is influenced by light and dark, as well as other factors. Our brain receives signals based on our environment and activates certain hormones, alters our body temperature, and regulates our metabolism to keep us alert or draw us into sleep.

Our circadian rhythm is our body's natural way of keeping to its 24-hour body clock, helping our body operate on a healthy sleep-wake schedule. Living a healthy, active lifestyle that promotes proper rest will help maintain this important component of our body.

How do circadian rhythms work?

Cells in our brain respond to light and dark. Our eyes capture such changes in the environment and then send signals to different cells about when it's time to be sleepy or awake. Those cells then send more signals to other parts of the brain, which activate other functions that make us more tired or alert. Hormones like melatonin and cortisol may increase or decrease as part of our circadian rhythm. Melatonin, as already explained, is the hormone that makes us sleepy, and our body releases more of it at night and suppresses it during the day. Cortisol can make us more alert, and our body produces more of it in the morning.

Body temperature and metabolism are also part of our circadian rhythm. Our temperature drops when we sleep and rises during awake hours. Additionally, our metabolism works at different rates throughout the day.

Other factors may also influence our circadian rhythm, such as our work hours, - working night shifts, - physical activity, stress and anxiety, and additional habits or lifestyle choices. Age is another factor, with infants, teens, and adults all experiencing circadian rhythms differently. And jet-lag is another example of our body's natural biological rhythm being thrown out of sync from its usual pattern.

Dr. Rick Strassman is an American clinical associate professor of psychiatry at the University of New Mexico School of Medicine. He has held a fellowship in clinical psychopharmacology research at the University of California San Diego and was Professor of Psychiatry for eleven years at the University of New Mexico. After 20 years of intermission, Strassman was the first person in the United States to undertake human research with psychedelic, hallucinogenic, or entheogenic substances with his research on dimethyltryptamine, - DMT. He is also the author of '*DMT: The Spirit Molecule*', which summarizes his academic research into DMT and other experimental studies of it, and includes his own reflections and conclusions based on this research.

Strassman's interest in the human biology of altered states of consciousness led him to study the pineal gland hormone melatonin in the 1980s, at which time there were suggestive data regarding its psychoactive effects. This research took place at the University of New Mexico's School of Medicine in Albuquerque,

17

where he became a tenured associate professor of psychiatry. He first developed a model of all-night suppression of melatonin by all-night bright light. He then established a successful exogenous melatonin infusion protocol that replicated endogenous melatonin levels in the bright-light conditions. All-night bright-light suppression of melatonin suppressed the normal trough of body temperature seen between 3-4 a.m., the time of maximum melatonin levels. Exogenous infusion of melatonin, replicating endogenous levels in the bright-light condition - in which endogenous melatonin was suppressed - reestablished the normal core body temperature trough. But melatonin's psychoactive effects were only sedative, leading him to focus on DMT in his future work.

From 1990 to 1995, Strassman led a government-funded clinical research team at the University of New Mexico studying the effects of dimethyltryptamine, - DMT - also on human subjects in experimental conditions. The research continued from his work on melatonin.

Strassman's studies between 1990 and 1995 aimed to experimentally investigate DMT's effects. As already mentioned, DMT is a powerful psychedelic drug found in hundreds of plants and every mammal that has been studied. It is made primarily in mammalian lung tissue and is related to serotonin and melatonin.

As a result of his research, Strassman came to call DMT the *'spirit molecule'* because its effects include many features of religious experience, such as visions, voices, disembodied consciousness, powerful emotions, novel insights, and feelings of overwhelming significance. During the project's five years, he administered approximately 400 doses of DMT to nearly 60 human volunteers. Strassman was the first in 20 years to legally administer psychedelics to people in the United States, and his research has widely been regarded as kicking off the *'psychedelic renaissance'*, in which many psychedelic compounds have begun to be scientifically studied for the first time since the early 1970s.

More than half of Strassman's volunteers reported profound encounters/interaction with nonhuman beings while in a dissociated state. Strassman has conjectured that when a person is approaching death or possibly when in a dream state, the body releases a relatively large amount of DMT, mediating some of the imagery survivors of near-death experiences report. But there are no data correlating endogenous DMT activity to non-drug-related altered states of consciousness. He also has theorised that the pineal gland may form DMT under certain conditions. In 2013 researchers first reported DMT in the pineal gland microdialysate of rodents.

Inspired by visions he had when he took LSD in the early 1970s, Strassman began studying Buddhism as a young man. He trained for 20 years in Zen Buddhism, received lay ordination in a Western Buddhist order, and led a meditation group of the order.

Some of Strassman's experimental participants say that other entities can resemble creatures more like insects and aliens than anything in the Bible. As a result, Strassman wrote that these experiences of his experimental participants *also left me feeling confused and concerned about where the spirit molecule was leading us. It was at this point that I began to wonder if I was getting in over my head with this research.* He has also hypothesized that endogenous DMT experiences could be the cause of alien abduction experiences.

DMT is released from the pineal gland during extraordinary states such as the time of death and the time of birth. So this gland may be the mechanism from which we enter and leave our physical bodies. This demonstrates the fact that DMT acts as a *'bridge'* between the physical body and the spiritual world. And it is the pineal gland that produces it!

So the pineal gland for sure is no ordinary organ! It has a greater role to play in our metaphysical and spiritual dimension! And meditation can activate this organ to its full potential.

We use so much energy through our eyes, but here is a 3rd Eye which is observing what our eyes are looking at and what our mind is thinking about. - It is indeed our biological clock!

Chapter 3:

Significance of Chakras

We are spiritual beings having a physical experience for this life-time. So we are both spiritual and physical, part of the great Cosmic Energy. And as physical beings, we have 5 physical senses - sight, hearing, smell, taste and touch, - all of which connect us to the physical, external world around us, and enable us to experience physicality. But what about our spiritual connection?

We have 7 main chakras, invisible spinning discs of energy, each having a different colour and function, aligned vertically from the base of our spine up to our crown, and these connect us with all things spiritual. On a personal level, well-balanced chakras can result in greater insight, improved health, and optimal well-being in all facets of life.

The word Chakra is the Sanskrit word for '*wheel*' or '*wheel of light*' and they are essentially the energy centres of the body, distributing life energy or cosmic energy in a consistent flow, balancing and harmonising the mind, body and spirit for maximum health and wellbeing. And just as the blood in the physical body flows through veins and arteries, so too, our chakra system distributes cosmic energy to various areas in the body through pathways called meridians. And it is these same meridians that are used in the practice of acupuncture to unblock trapped energy and increase the energy flow.

Each chakra vibrates at a specific energy frequency level, and so each is associated with the specific colour or musical note with which each chakra resonates best, so increasing its energy. And as we have seen, each chakra is associated with a particular and specific body gland.

These 7 chakras can be extended to include 5 more as we progress on our spiritual path and encompass higher centres of energy in our being, - bringing us to 12 chakras in total. And the amazing thing is that we have never been taught about any of our chakras in our education systems!

For those people who are aware of their chakras, the 7-chakra-system is the one which is the most familiar. The first 3 chakras are known as the lower chakras, - the base, sacral and solar plexus as they are related to the physical realm, connecting us with the physical material world around us. Even though they are known as the '*lower*' chakras, they are of no less significance than the '*higher*' chakras - the heart, throat, 3rd Eye and crown chakras. They all need to be in alignment and balance, and spinning at the same rate in order for us to progress on our spiritual journey.

The **Base** or **Root Chakra**, - ***Muladhara, -*** coloured red, at the base of the spine, '*grounds*' us in this material physical world, in our own self, in our feeling of belonging, our sense of identity. It is this chakra that connects us to our material needs, - food, family, shelter, safety, money, etc and everything we require for our physical survival on Planet Earth. It is associated with the ***gonads gland***, - relating to the kidneys, testes and spine.

When this Root Chakra is balanced and working to optimum level, we feel grounded, confident, safe, stable and secure in our physical reality, comfortable in our own skin, physically healthy, prosperous, able to be still, and able to be present in the here and now.

When this Root Chakra is congested or blocked, we feel anxious, restless and fearful, flighty, underweight, fatigued, unmotivated, resistant to structure and have difficulty manifesting.

When this Root Chakra is overstimulated, we feel heavy and sluggish, greedy, overeating, hoarding, resistant to change, too much focused on material things, overspending, possibly a workaholic, maybe obsessing over money or physical health.

The Sacral Chakra, - *Swadhisthana*, - coloured orange, is located below the navel, and is the energy centre from where we feel pleasure and passion, from where our thoughts of creativity and joy emerge, and from where our feelings of abundance are stimulated. This is our reproductive, sexuality and creativity chakra, governing our desires, likes and what brings us joy and fulfilment in life. We all carry both masculine and feminine energies within us, - which have nothing to do with our biological sex or gender. It is the Divine Feminine energy within us that is related to sensuality and sexuality, creativity, procreation and pleasure. Represented by the water element, this feminine energy is also affected by the power of the moon.

The sacral chakra is associated with the ***lymphatic system***, - the bladder, gall blader, prostate, spleen, ovaries and kidney.

When this Sacral Chakra is balanced and working to optimum level, we are able to embrace change, we are emotionally intelligent, nurturing of self and others, passionate about what we do, able to enjoy pleasure, have healthy boundaries, and sexual satisfaction. We are living true to ourself!

When this Sacral Chakra is congested or blocked, we feel rigid in our body, our beliefs or our behaviour, bored, lacking stimulus, blocked or stuck in some way, emotionally numb or insensitive, fearful of change, lacking in desire, passion or excitement, avoiding pleasure, fearful of our sexuality, have excessive boundaries, and poor social skills.

When this Sacral Chakra is overstimulated, we feel obsessive tendencies or attachments with poor boundaries, emotional dependency and invasion of others, sexual addictions and addiction to stimulants. We experience feelings of instability, excessive mood swings, we are excessively sensitive, and needful of attention.

The **Solar Plexus Chakra, - Manipura, -** coloured yellow, is just below the belly button between the heart and sacral chakra. This chakra is often referred to as the '*human rubbish dump*', and can often feel like a churning cement mixer, simply because it is the Solar Plexus that is the seat of our self-esteem and confidence, and where we harbour and store our emotions, - hurts, fears, triumphs, successes, and our feelings of worthiness or unworthiness. This is where the ego resides. And this is where our sense of self is nourished.

The solar plexus is associated with the **adrenal glands**, relating to the upper spine, stomach, bladder, kidneys, intestines, pancreas and liver.

When this Solar Plexus Chakra is in full working order, we feel responsible, with good self-discipline, reliable, confident, energetic, spontaneous, generous, warm, compassionate and humorous. Being confident in our own person, we do not let other people's negative opinions or views influence us.

When this Solar Plexus is blocked or congested, we feel a sense of unease in our stomach, as if there is something we literally just '*cannot stomach*'. We feel weak-willed, passive and submissive, insecure, powerless, lacking in energy and confidence with low self-esteem, and poor digestion, possibly heartburn or ulcers.

When this Solar Plexus is overstimulated, we feel

controlling, aggressive and domineering, arrogant, competitive, ambitious and driven, hyperactive, stubborn, maybe even jealous, greedy, envious of the success of others, dismissing them or putting them down, and attracted to sedatives. Indeed, while many of these behaviours might appear to suggest confidence, they are really strong signs of insecurity.

The Heart Chakra, - *Anahata,* - coloured green, is in the centre of the chest, the centre of our being. It is the source of self-love, the love we express to other people and to all other forms of life. This chakra governs our relationships and our human connections, stimulating our love energy, and pure unconditional love. Pure unconditional love is the highest vibration in the entire energy spectrum, where we see the Oneness in the totality of All That Is, - meaning that we see ourselves, first of all, and then every other person and form of life as the pure spiritual beings we all are, and so we do not judge, we do not criticise, we do not condemn, but instead, we accept and embrace all diversities and differences with openness and understanding. We cannot, however, act only from our heart and our emotions! We need to balance the intellect with the emotions!

The heart chakra is associated with the **thymus gland**, relating to the lungs and heart.

When this Heart Chakra is operating at optimum level, we are caring, compassionate, empathetic, accepting, self-loving, peaceful, content, and able to connect with others even during difficult times.

When this Heart Chakra is blocked or congested, we are withdrawn, anti-social, critical and intolerant, isolated and lonely, fearful of intimacy, and lacking in empathy.

When this Heart Chakra is overstimulated, we have poor boundaries with co-dependency and focusing too much on others, we are being a martyr, trying to please others, we experience jealousy.

The **Throat Chakra, - *Vishuddhi*, -** coloured blue, is located at the throat, and governs our communication systems, - our ability to speak, to express ourselves, to listen and to communicate through to higher spiritual beings. It is through the Throat Chakra that we live our truth, aligned with our authentic selves.

The throat chakra is associated with the **thyroid gland,** relating to the vocal cords, bronchia, oesophagus, mouth and tongue and respiratory tract.

When this Throat Chakra is working properly, we have clear communication with others and with ourself, we are a good listener, we can give full voice to our feelings and our sense of who we are, speaking our mind openly, confidently and honestly. We have the courage to express ourselves and what we believe in, even when faced with challenges, hostility and negativity. And it is through the Heart Chakra that we express gratitude for everything we have got. So when our Heart Chakra is working properly, we give thanks for absolutely everything, - including what might appear to be negative, because we see the positive and the lesson it might well carry.

When this Throat Chakra is blocked or congested, we have difficulty expressing ourself in words, fearful of speaking, secretive, excessively shy and not hearing what we need to hear. We often keep quiet in order just to keep the peace, or tell others what we think they want to hear, again just to avoid conflict or criticism. Our lack of faith in ourself and our feelings of inadequacy can mean we cannot express our needs in front of others, and so cannot question or call others to account. And when we cannot adequately express our feelings, then this in turn leads to other ailments such as depression and withdrawal from society. We see nothing to be grateful for, - only doom and gloom all around.

When this Throat Chakra is overstimulated, we are talking too much, gossiping, or speaking inappropriately, we are excessively loud, and we cannot keep confidences. We are aggressive and domineering in conversations, always wanting to dictate the topic.

The **Third Eye Chakra**, *Agna,* - coloured indigo, and as we have seen, is located at the centre of the forehead, between the two eyebrows, and is connected to the *pineal gland*, relating to the eyes, brain, and also, the pituitary gland. As we have seen too, this chakra governs your intuition, deeper inner wisdom, deeper insight, higher consciousness and greater awareness. It is all about understanding the true nature of reality and not the distorted version of reality we see with our two physical eyes.

When this Third Eye Chakra is working to full capacity, we feel strongly intuitive, with penetrating insight and creative imagination, good memory, good dream recall, ability to visualise, seeing beyond what our two physical eyes see.

When this Third Eye Chakra is blocked or congested, we lack imagination and have difficulty visualising, we are insensitive, experiencing excessive scepticism, unable to see alternatives and in denial.

When this Third Eye Chakra is overstimulated, we experience hallucinations, delusions, nightmares, intrusive memories and fantasising, and we have difficulty concentrating.

The **Crown Chakra, - *Sahasrara,* -** coloured violet or purple, is located right at the top of the head and is associated with the ***pituitary gland***, relating to our brain stem and full spinal cord. This chakra, sometimes referred to as the '*bridge'*, governs our link to the Divine and the higher levels of consciousness. It is also known as the door to enlightenment.

When this Crown Chakra is functioning properly, we are spiritually connected, open minded, able to question, assimilate, and analyse information, wise and intelligent. We experience a state that is entirely beyond the physical realms.

When this Crown Chakra is blocked or congested, we have a closed mind, difficulty learning and processing information, rigid belief systems, apathy, spiritual cynicism. Headaches and problems relating to our physical vision can also be the result of this chakra being blocked, as can an acute awareness of the conflicts in the world.

When this Crown Chakra is overstimulated, we feel dissociated from our body, confused, living *'in your head',* disconnected from spirit, and with excessive attachments and over-intellectualisation.

So, as we can see, each of these chakras corresponds to a particular spiritual function, and each manifests its energy through different ways.

The chakras are indeed barometers of physical, mental and spiritual health. - That's how significant they are! They are our spiritual connection to the One Great Universal Energy we call God, to ALL THAT IS.

And the 3rd Eye is the 6th chakra.

Chapter 4:

Why it is necessary to activate your 3rd Eye, - advantages in your life

We have seen in a previous chapter how important and significant our pineal gland is, and as our pineal gland relates to and is associated with our 3rd Eye chakra, then that means that our 3rd Eye is of utmost importance too! And not just as a deeply spiritual concept, but also as a vital mechanism in our overall physical health and wellbeing.

The parts of our brain associated with the 3rd Eye also include the hypothalamus and the pituitary gland. And these are usually associated with mental health, vision, sleep and spiritual awareness. The pineal gland, as we have also previously seen, is responsible for regulating our sleep-wake patterns, by secreting and regulating melatonin, and when these sleep-wake patterns are regular, our circadian rhythms are normal. And when our circadian rhythms, - our internal sensory biological mechanism, - is in order, then we experience good physical and mental health, while avoiding stress and anxiety in our life. So it is not rocket science, nor does one need to be the Brain of Britain to work out that activating our 3rd Eye is the key to good health!

The pineal gland is strongly prone to calcification, which is a build-up, over time, of calcium, phosphorus and fluoride. Calcification of the pineal gland is basically where a hard, solid ridge builds up around the gland, effectively blocking access to other realms, and is more likely to occur when the 3rd Eye is dormant. Hence, the majority of people today have some degree of calcification in the pineal gland. An awakened or active 3rd Eye keeps the pineal gland healthy, and prevents calcification from occurring.

So! Obviously, it is necessary to activate our 3rd Eye! And why? To repeat! - Simply because our 3rd Eye in turn keeps our pineal gland healthy! And our pineal gland in turn produces melatonin which keeps our body's sleep cycle and circadian rhythm in order. Low melatonin production by our pineal gland can often lead to a lethargic thyroid, to headaches, osteoporosis, nausea, to mood swings, fatigue, depression and even mental disorders, to issues with sense of direction, to poor blood circulation, kidney or digestive disorders, to confusion and to spiritual disconnection. So, if we want to avoid any of these in our life, then it is certainly to our great advantage to activate our 3rd Eye. - No argument there!

And the good news? The good news is that it is always possible to decalcify an already calcified pineal gland. How? By dissolving the build-up of calcium, fluoride and phosphate that has accumulated over the years. And how do we do that?

Let us see!

Chapter 5:

Decalcifying the pineal gland

As in all spiritual traditions, the '*vision*' of the third eye plays a fundamental role in the connection of the Spirit with man. In fact, it allows us to enter the '*non-material*' world, of the apparently invisible, through extra-sensorial perception, to bring us knowledge, deep awareness and '*guide*' our existence.

This is why it is so important to keep that pineal gland, - our 3rd Eye, - active and in a functional state. Due to the accumulation of toxins and heavy metals in the human body over time, such as fluoride, aluminium and mercury, the 3rd Eye becomes calcified, and gradually inactive. Hence the highlighting by activist groups of the dangers of the amount of fluoride that is being put into our waters! Fluoride is probably the element that most speeds up the decreasing functionality of our 3rd Eye. It is found in food products, and in such as toothpaste and mouthwashes, in chewing gum, and in fizzy drinks.

We can detoxify our body and take substances that promote the decalcification of the pineal gland. This is important because in order to achieve higher states of consciousness, toxins must first be cleansed from the body and one must become grounded to the energy of the earth. Opening or activating the third eye is a practice that anyone can do. It is not in any way dangerous, but like all spiritual practices, it takes time and cannot be hurried or forced. It is best done through meditation, with the focus totally on that area of the forehead.

We can decalcify our pineal gland and help to keep it decalcified by the following methods:

- Avoid excessive intake of calcium. Yes, calcium is important for our overall health and for maintaining strong bones and teeth. But most people consume too much calcium, either in food or in calcium supplements. Natural sources of calcium include dairy products, seafood, nuts and seeds and legumes. But all in moderation!

- Avoid excessive fluoride. Most of our intake of fluoride comes from the water flowing through our taps, - the water supplies of our cities and towns contain enormous amounts of fluoride. So drink alternative forms of water, or use a special filter to remove the fluoride from your drinking water. Toothpaste too is a source of fluoride. So read the label before you buy, or use baking soda every other day.

- Avoid fluorescent lighting. The pineal gland is very sensitive to light and functions best in natural lighting. Fluorescent light bulbs are not part of the natural light spectrum and so are detrimental to a healthy pineal gland.

- Avoid mercury tooth fillings. Mercury is an extremely toxic heavy metal, and used in tooth fillings so near to the brain, can cause problems in the pineal gland.

- Increase your intake of organic food. The heavy metals in pesticides used in agriculture and crop production are all detrimental to the health of the pineal gland. Grass-fed sources of meat and organic poultry are also highly recommended. Buy your eggs from where you can see the hens taking in the natural vitamins from the soil in the earth.

- Expose yourself to the sun. The orange healing rays of the sun during sunrise or sunset are extremely beneficial to a healthy pineal gland.

Taking a walk or sitting outdoors at at these times can certainly help to keep the pineal gland healthy.

- Use bentonite clay, - a type of clay formed by volcanic ash and which has been used throughout history for detoxifying properties. Bentonite clay has magnetic properties that attract and bind with toxins, especially heavy metals and removes them from the body. Hence masks or massages using bentonite clay are often offered in health spas and beauty parlours.

- Practise yoga. The word '*yoga*' comes from the Sanskrit word '*yog*' or '*jog*', meaning '*to unify*', - unifying our human consciousness and the One Great Universal Consciousness we call God. And this is the very same aim of awakening the 3rd Eye! The practice of yoga is a way of life and not just something we do as part of our fitness regime or mindfulness programme. If you are practising yoga in the morning, do so on an empty stomach, and if in the afternoon or evening, leave at least four to five hours since your last meal. If you experience any sharp pain or great discomfort at any time during your yoga practice, then you should consult your doctor.

- Practise seeing the aura. Soften your vision, - don't squint! Start with observing mountain tops, flowers, trees, etc. Again, this too takes patience and practice!

- Use 3rd Eye colours in your home. The colour indigo, as we have seen previously, is a combination of the two colours violet and deep blue, so surround yourself with hues of indigo, purple and blue in your home or work place, not just in light furnishings, but also on walls and heavy furniture. Incorporate them also into your wardrobe and the clothes and jewellery you wear.

- Use essential oils, either in a diffuser, in the bath, or in aromatherapy or massage. Essential oils have calming, energising and pain-relieving qualities, calming anxiety, alleviating depression, promoting sleep and increasing focus and concentration. The best oils for the 3rd £ye chakra include chamomile, lavender, myrrh, sandalwood, nutmeg and grapefruit.

- Crystals and stones contain vibrational energy that resonates with the various chakras. For the

3rd Eye chakra, the best include amethyst for healing and wisdom; purple fluoride for clarity and enhanced intuition; azurite for developing psychic abilities; black obsidian for balancing the 3rd Eye chakra; lapis lazuli, a beautiful blue crystal used widely in ancient Egypt, for healing and calming; sodalite for stimulating the pineal gland, developing psychic powers and promoting clarity and intuition; indigo kyanite for developing psychic gifts and balancing the whole chakra system; moldavite for clearing negative thoughts and cleansing all of the chakras.

- Empower your mind with affirmations! When repeated over and over again, the brain comes to believe they are true. Slogans and repetitions have always been used down through history as a tool to influence how people think and believe and hence how they act. For the 3rd Eye chakra, affirmations should focus on insight and intuition. Examples could include: *'I am insightful and intuitive'; 'I trust my intuition and follow it at all times'; 'I expand my awareness through my 3rd Eye'; 'I am open to the wisdom of my 3rd Eye'; 'I am connected with my Higher Self'; 'I trust that my life is unfolding just as it should'; 'My 3rd Eye is developing all the time'; 'I am in alignment with divine universal wisdom'.*

The old saying *'You are what you eat!'* certainly applies to the health of the pineal gland. The food we eat is of utmost importance in keeping our pineal gland healthy. So let us now talk about food and diet!

Nourishing foods:

It is important that we keep a balance of energy in our body.

Ayurveda is an alternative medicine system with historical roots in the Indian subcontinent. The Sanskrit term *'āyurveda'* is composed of two words, *'āyus,'* meaning *'life'* or *'longevity',* and *'veda',* meaning *'knowledge',* and altogether translated as *'knowledge of longevity'* or *'knowledge of life and longevity'.*

Ultimately, Ayurveda seeks to reduce disease, particularly those that are chronic, and increase positive health in the body and mind. It is heavily practised in India and Nepal, where around 80% of the population report using it. In Ayurveda texts, dosha balance is emphasized, and suppressing natural urges is

considered unhealthy and claimed to lead to illness.
The Sanskrit word *'Dosha'* is a central term in Ayurveda,
translated as *'that which can cause problems'*, - literally
meaning *'fault'* or *'defect'*, - and which refers to three
categories or types of substances that are believed to
be present conceptually in a person's body and mind.
These Dosha are assigned specific qualities and
functions. These qualities and functions are affected by
external and internal stimuli received by the body.

Ayurveda treatises describe three elemental doshas, -
vata, pitta and kapha, and state that balance of the
doshas results in health, while imbalance results in
disease. The Ayurvedic notion of doshas describes how
bad habits, wrong diet, overwork, etc., may cause
relative deficiencies or excesses which cause them to
become imbalanced in relation to the natural
constitution, which may result in mental, nervous, and
digestive disorders, including low energy and
weakening of all body tissues.

Excess of pitta is blamed for blood toxicity,
inflammation, and infection. Excess of kapha is blamed
for increase in mucus, weight, oedema, and lung
disease, etc. And excess of vata is blamed for pain in
the body, - pain being the characteristic feature of
deranged vata. Some of the diseases connected to

unbalanced vata are flatulence, gout, rheumatism, etc.

And food, in Ayurveda, is classified into three main categories, based on their effect on our energies, - sattva, rajas and tamas. Generally speaking, consumption of rajasic and tamasic foods should be limited, due to how they produce excess amounts of energy in the body, manifesting in irritability, restlessness, anger, sleeplessness, and hyperactivity, - all of which can block our 3rd Eye.

Examples of rajasic foods, which can lead to toxicity in the blood and make us feel heavier and sluggish, include fried foods, sour milk and cream, alcoholic or carbonated drinks, chocolate, coffee, foods containing meat and fish, foods containing salt, mustard or strong flavours such as garlic, vinegar, chilies, onions, pickles, etc.

Examples of tamasic foods, which also make us feel lazy, tired and lethargic, include chips and french fries, artificially flavoured and processed foods like jam and jellies, canned and tinned foods, refined sugar and flour, milk and cheeses that are either highly pasteurised or kept in very cold temperatures.

And what about the sattvic diet plan? Sattvic foods are

definitely the best foods for anyone wanting to cleanse not just their 3rd Eye chakra, but all the chakras. In contrast to the heavy textures of the rajasic and tamasic foods, sattvic foods are natural, light, fresh and uncontaminated by additives or artificial flavours.

Examples of sattvic foods include fresh fruit and fruit juices, fresh leafy green vegetables, nuts and seeds, - especially such as almonds and pumpkin, grains such as brown rice, wheat, oats and legumes, fresh milk, buttermilk, yogurt, butter, olive, sesame or coconut oil, raw sugar or honey for sweetening, fresh spices such as cinnamon, poppy, mugwort, turmeric, coriander, ginger, fennel, lavender, dill, juniper, thyme, rosemary, mint, etc.

Adherence to a sustained sattvic diet results in energy and balance within the body at all times. So basically, avoid heavy processed food, including meat and meat products, as these animals die in trauma and carry heavy energy. Avoid too all processed foods, as these contain chemicals and foreign substances, including refined sugar, salt and saturated fats, - all of which create an imbalance in our subtle energies.

And finally to end this chapter, - remember how we read earlier about the importance of colours and how each colour carries a particular energy vibration?

And the colour associated with the 3rd Eye? - Indigo!
Verging on purple!

So to keep your 3rd Eye healthy, focus on foods that are
indigo, violet, dark blue or deep purple in colour. These
are all good for the pineal gland, and in turn, for the 3rd
Eye chakra. The colour pigments in these foods are said
to represent dreams, inner thoughts, and inner
harmony within the universe.

They are also great for regulating blood pressure and
are powerful antioxidants that keep your brain
performing at optimum health. These include purple
grapes, blueberries, prunes, purple figs, blackberries,
raisins, raw cacoa, plums, dates, eggplants and all
purple-coloured variations of vegetables such as purple
kale, purple cabbage, purple onions, etc. Dark
chocolate, - NOT white or milk chocolate! - enhances
brain clarity and contains serotonin, which as we have
seen, is a mood-boosting hormone.

And increase your intake of foods that activate the
decalcification process. Foods such as bananas,
avocados, pineapple, cucumber, watercress for
example, are all a healthy choice for a healthy pineal

gland, while meat, and especially pork and beef are highly acidic and not conducive to brain health in general. Apple cider vinegar, - either in liquid form or tablet, - iodine, spirulina, chlorella are also great for decalsifying and preventing further calcification from forming. Use healing herbs such as parsley, dill, mugwort, oregano, alfalfa either in salads, stews, dips, or include them in your water drinks or as herbal teas. Nuts and seeds contain powerful brain nutrients that help with focus and clarity. Pumkin seeds and almonds are especially recommended. Fish contains Omega-3 fatty acids, another great brain nutrient that enhances attention and concentration. Eat fish at least twice a week when you are working on opening your 3rd Eye and once a week after that. Herbs and spices maintain nervous system health and enhance the senses. Poppy seeds, mugwort, juniper, rosemary and mint are especially potent. Turmeric has been used since ancient times as well to promote overall brain health. And of course - drink plenty of filtered water, do physical exercise, and spend time in nature!

And follow the sattvic diet!

Your pineal gland and 3rd Eye will thank you for it!

Chapter 6:

TECHNIQUES AND EXERCISES FOR AWAKENING AND ACTIVATING The 3rd EYE

First of all, we must remember that as the pineal gland is closely associated with our eyes and head, it is always better to keep our eyes healthy.

Eye exercises:

Here are a few exercises and ideas to strengthen the muscles which are holding your eyeballs:

- Look at your palm at a close distance and then look at some object which is far from you, looking back and forth 30-50 times.

- Rotate and roll your eyes from right to left, and left to right. Roll your eyes to your shoulders, to your right shoulder and then to your left.

- Look at the tip of your nose, rolling your eyes.

- Look at the centre of your forehead - all the time rolling your eyes.

- Spend time in nature. And observe!

- Do not use mobile phones, computers, etc. at least one hour before you go to sleep.

Activating your 3rd Eye:

Having seen how important and significant your 3rd Eye actually is, let us now begin to activate it! Remember, it has been closed for most of your life, so it will take time and practice, but with time, practice, patience and perseverance, it will happen!

Wherever your attention goes, and whatever part of your body you focus on, then that part of the body starts functioning better. So sit in meditative pose, close your eyes and bring your awareness to your forehead region, by rolling your eyes upwards and inwards towards where your 3rd Eye rests. Stay in this position, where you are internally looking at this spot. In the beginning you might have a little headache, but with practice you will feel comfortable. So rolling your eyes, stay in this position for some time. You might see a large eye, which can be either open or closed. It is hard to hold the vision at first for any length of time, so if you lose it, open your eyes, then close them and begin again.

Initial exercises to start increasing awareness:

Opening the 3rd Eye is all about seeing beyond what the two physical eyes allow us to see, which as we have learned throughout this book, is very limited indeed! We are all part of the Oneness, - the Oneness of the One Great Universal Energy we call God, the Oneness of the totality of All That Is. The Cosmic Hologram! The microcosms contained within the macrocosm! I am in everything, and everything else is in me.

So, here are a few simple exercises to start you off on your path:

- You are driving past a field of sheep. Your two physical eyes see the sheep. But when you tune into your 3rd Eye? - What is it telling you? Your 3rd Eye is urging you to see the Oneness. Those sheep are me. I am those sheep. So in what way do I express the behaviours of the sheep? Am I just following other people in my life? Am I not going in my own preferred and individual direction in life? In what way am I just following the crowd?

- A magpie flies past you. Your two physical eyes see the magpie. But when you tune into your 3rd Eye? - What is it telling you? Your 3rd Eye is urging you to see the Oneness. That magpie is me. I am that magpie. So in what way do I express the behaviours of the magpie? Do I collect and hoard material possessions? Do I gather things just because they glitter, sparkle and shine?

- You watch the birds feeding. Your two eyes are seeing the birds feeding. But when you tune into your 3rd Eye? - What is it telling you? Your 3rd Eye is urging you to see how the birds take only what they need at this moment in time. And why? Simply because their trust in the Universe is such that they know more food will appear as and when they need it. Do I trust in the Universe to provide me with what I need? Am I taking more than my fair share because I fear there will not be enough for me?

- You watch a tortoise slowly moving along. Your two eyes see the tortoise. But your 3rd Eye? What is your 3rd Eye telling you? Your 3rd Eye is telling you the tortoise always gets there in the end! Why am I always in such a hurry? Why am I always rushing? I need to slow down!

- You watch a parrot. The parrot prattles away! But sayingand repeating only what others say - and mostly rubbish! Nothing individual or original! What is your 3rd Eye telling you? - Am I just repeating what other people say? Have I lost my own voice to others?

- The cuckoo! Everyone listens for the cuckoo song in Spring. Your two physical eyes see the cuckoo. But when you tune into your 3rd Eye? - What is it telling you? Your 3rd Eye is urging you to see the Oneness. That cuckoo is me. I am that cuckoo. So in what way do I express the behaviours of the cuckoo? The cuckoo lays its eggs in the nests of other birds. So in what ways am I using other people to do my work for me? Manipulating them? Avoiding my own responsibilities?

- You watch an ostrich hiding its head in the sand! What is your 3rd Eye telling you? - What am I trying to ignore? To avoid dealing with? To get away from? Pretending that if I don't see it, it will disappear?

- You watch the autumn leaves falling off the trees! Your two eyes see the magnificent kaleidoscope of colours. But what is your 3rd Eye telling you? - Your 3rd Eye is telling you that there must be an ending before there can be a new beginning! And how beautiful endings can be!

- You watch the trees bend and sway with the wind. What is your 3rd Eye telling you? - Go with the flow!

- You watch the river flowing. The tree is in its way! The water simply flows around the tree! What is your 3rd Eye telling you? - Do not try and knock down the obstacles I encounter in life! Circumnavigate them! Find a way around them!

- Watch your pet! How it never shows disapproval or criticism of you! Synonymous with unconditional love! What is your 3rd Eye telling you? - The difference in animals and humans? - Animals know how to love! - I need to accept all diversities and differences without criticism or judgement!

- Watch children playing. They may be of a different skin colour, they may speak a different language. What is your 3rd Eye telling you? - That they nevertheless find a way to communicate and play together!

We often see and recognise various signs from the Universe. But! This does not mean that the Universe has deliberately set out to send us that particular sign! It just means that we are seeing through our 3rd Eye! All those signs have been around us all along, but we have been seeing with just our two physical eyes!

The Universe is NOT sending you a sheep or a magpie! It is simply your 3rd Eye tuning you into your surroundings! Into the Oneness!

And when the doorbell rings or the phone rings, and lo and behold! - There is that person you were just thinking about! What has happened here? This is synchronicity at work! This is your 3rd Eye at work! The Universe has done nothing spectacular - because, remember! Everything is within yourself! In other words, whatever you are looking for, is already inside you! But you are now seeing through the lens of your 3rd Eye. And that's what makes the difference! - **_Inner vision_**!

Exercises and techniques for activating your 3rd Eye:

Now let us move further and delve deeper!

- **Touching the 3rd Eye**: The purpose of this exercise is to enforce the intention of the subconscious. Place your finger on your 3rd Eye chakra in the middle of your forehead and silently state the intention of awakening it. Gently massage your third eye in a circular motion and visualise it beginning to pulse and awaken. Continue for 3-4 minutes. Pause every few seconds to gently tap on the 3rd Eye   two or three times, then continue massaging, visualising the eye as it slowly begins to awaken under your touch

- **Crystal exercises:** Certain stones and crystals help energise the 3rd Eye chakra, for example amethyst, lapis lazuli, blue sapphire, blue agate, blue quartz. Pick up the stone or crystal and hold it in your hand for a moment, sensing and feeling its energy. Now close your eyes and visualise the energy flowing from the crystal to your 3rd Eye chakra. Feel it enter your 3rd Eye chakra, warming it and causing it to tingle or pulsate. Practise this exercise with a different stone each time, letting your intuition guide you as to which one you choose

- **Crystal meditation:** Lie down and place an amethyst on your 3rd Eye. Visualise the energy from the crystal penetrating your 3rd Eye and filling it with energy. Silently state the intention that you are awakening your 3rd Eye. Continue for as long as you wish

- **Colour visualisation**: All colours are an energy vibration, and this visualisation of purple or dark blue on your 3rd Eye is one of the best exercises for energising and unblocking the 3rd Eye chakra. Sit in a comfortable position, and take three deep breaths, allowing the tension to leave your body. Close your eyes and visualise a purple or dark blue wheel of energy spinning in the area of your 3rd Eye. Focus on the ball of energy as it radiates energy into your 3rd Eye. Continue for as long as you wish

- **Third Eye Visualisation:** This exercise requires extreme concentration, but like all the other exercises here, over time it will become easier. It works to awaken your inner eye by using it to replace your two physical eyes. Start with simple objects until your 3rd Eye is trained to do this with more complex objects. An image of a circle, square, or a circle in a vivid colour is a good example to start with. You can also choose any simple physical object such as a pen, a book cover, etc. Stare at the object intently for a few minutes, registering every detail. Close your eyes and visualise the object, recreating every detail and colour you can see until you can see it in your mind's eye as if you are viewing it physically with your two eyes

- **Mindfulness Grounding Exercise:** One of the main causes of a dormant 3rd Eye is not living mindfully and not being grounded in the present. But the present is all there is! The past has gone, and the future never actually materialises, because when tomorrow or next week or next year comes, it is now the present! We all tend to think too much about the future and the past, and we all tend to live in some sort of fantasy world, and all of this causes our 3rd Eye to lose perspective because it is not grounded in reality. You can apply this exercise to anything you do in daily life: - eating a meal, washing the dishes, cleaning, or any other mundane task. Rather than letting your mind wander, focus only on what you are doing, using ALL your senses! And focusing like this and using all your senses is key to keeping your 3rd Eye grounded in reality!

- **Visualising a Golden Ball of Light:** Sit in the lotus position or on a comfortable chair with your back straight. Breathe deeply and feel the tension leave your body with every breath. Now visualise a warm stream of energy flowing through your body from the top of your head down to your toes. Continue to visualise and feel this energy slowly circulating around your body. Next, direct your focus to the 3rd Eye chakra and the warm space between your brows. Visualise the energy coming together to form a rotating ball of golden light in the centre of your 3rd Eye chakra. Focus on the rotating ball and the beautiful golden light that emanates from it. When you are ready, and only when you are ready, - this cannot be hurried, - allow this beautiful golden rotating light to expand until it fills all of your 3rd Eye chakra. Visualise it expanding slowly until it finally emerges out of your forehead in a bright ray of incandescent golden light. Gaze at the beautiful ray of light with your inner eye and notice any colours or pictures that appear within it. Simply acknowledge what you see without judgement. Take your time. When you are ready, and still gazing into the light with your 3rd Eye, ask your 3rd Eye if it has any messages for you. Take as much time as you need

Again, don't worry if you don't see anything the first few times. The more you advance, the stronger the ray of light will become as well as the images and messages from your 3rd Eye. Keep practising!

- **Body Scan Meditation for 3rd Eye Intuition**: This meditation is specifically geared toward increasing your intuition through the 3rd Eye chakra. It serves to heighten your intuition by making you more aware of the subtle sensations in all the different parts of you body. Sit in a comfortable position with your back straight. Close your eyes and do the mindful breathing exercise to ground yourself, for two to three minutes, or until all the tension is released from your body and you feel completely relaxed. Start the body scan from the very top of your head or the crown chakra. Focus on this area and tune into it until you begin to notice the sensations there. This could be tingling, throbbing, pulsing, pressure, a slight warmth, burning, or buzzing. Don't worry if you don't feel anything the first couple of times. Your mind will become trained to pick up on these sensations over time. When you are ready, move down to the forehead area from the front to the back of your head. Focus on this area, again noticing any sensations there. When you are ready, move down to the eyes, then the nose, the area above the mouth and then the mouth itself. Spend a few minutes on each area, and notice the sensations. Continue down to the chin, neck, shoulders, arms, torso, top of the stomach, lower belly, upper thighs, legs, and finally end with the feet. Do not react to or judge any negative sensations that you may feel. Simply acknowledge them and move on

- **Projection:** This wonderful exercise allows you to travel through time and space, - in your mind! It awakens your inner senses and gives your 3rd Eye a great work-out. Choose a place you know well and enjoy visiting, - a park, a shop you love, or your favourite restaurant for example. Close your eyes and visualise every detail, then try and imagine yourself in that place as if you were there physically. Relive a past event that happened in that place as if it is happening again at this very moment. Try to recall every detail and even the conversations you had. Let yourself be transported back into the past and play out the scene as if you had gone back in time. Now, project yourself into the future by imagining either that same place or another place you know well. Visualise what will happen the next time you visit that place, what you will be wearing, what the weather will be like, or people you will meet. Let your mind take you wherever it will, as you project yourself into that future scene

- **Meditation: 3rd Eye Awakening and Decalcifying the Pineal Gland**: This meditation energises both the 3rd Eye chakra and the pineal gland and heightens awareness and the senses. Sit in a comfortable position and allow your body a few minutes to settle and relax. Close your eyes, take a deep breath, and hold it for as long as you can, feeling the fulness in your lungs. Exhale slowly through your mouth. Bring your focus to your 3rd Eye chakra. If it helps, you can visualise it as a small ball of light. Allow your senses to become vividly and intensely aware of everything around you; any sounds in the background like voices or the hum of electrical appliances, the seat beneath you, the feel of your clothes against your skin, and any smells that may come to you. Allow your senses to fully experience all of these things while dismissing any thoughts about them. Visualise your 3rd Eye absorbing and processing all of these sounds, smells and sensations

- **African Tongue-Rolling:** This is a traditional practice among various tribes where communing with the spirit world is a sacred rite. They believe that the 3rd Eye chakra must be very powerful in order to engage in these rites, and hence this exercise is commonly practised to strengthen it. Use your tongue to slowly stroke the roof of your mouth from front to back for a few minutes. Now slide your tongue faster along the roof of your mouth and use your voice to make a fluttering sound. Feel the roof of your mouth begin to vibrate. Intensify the movement to increase the vibration as much as possible. This is supposed to *'attract the attention of the third eye'.* Continue doing this for 3-4 minutes

- **Moon-Gazing**: Moonlight energises the 3rd Eye, heightens intuition and sharpens perception, and this is a simple and relaxing way to promote silence of the mind while bathing your 3rd Eye in the nurturing, energising and revitalising rays of the moon. Sit or lie back in the rays of the moon, contemplating its wondrous beauty and the beauty of the stars. Imagine the moon's light bathing your body and entering into your 3rd Eye. Acknowledge any thoughts that come to you, and try to listen to your 3rd Eye.

- **Scrying:** This is an ancient practice of psychic awareness or second sight. It allows you to *'see'* in a similar way to a fortune-teller gazing into a crystal ball. It involves gazing into any medium, for example, a crystal, a mirror, water, fire or smoke. Staring into the flame of a candle or a wood fire is a great way to see amazing images and receive amazing messages. Sit comfortably and gaze intently at whatever you have chosen for the exercise. Gently relax your vision and allow it to become a little unfocused. Continue to stare into the mirror, water, fire or smoke until images begin to form. Contemplate the images and try to see if you can interpret any messages from your 3rd Eye. You may not necessarily see any clear visions or receive specific messages, especially at the beginning. The goal of scrying is to give you a sense of the psychic energy residing within your 3rd Eye, and the more you awaken it, the more vivid the images you receive will become - and the more easily you will be able to interpret them.

- **Practise seeing your aura**

- **Balasana Yoga Pose:** This is known as the *'Sleeping child'* or *'child's pose'* position. Sit on your heels and breathe deeply three times. Slowly lower your upper body forward until your forehead is touching the floor, keeping your arms lying next to your body, palms up, and not stretched out in front of you. Bring your awareness to your forehead and keep your focus and concentration there. Breathe deeply for a few minutes, focusing only on your forehead. Very slowly raise your body up again until you are back in the sitting position on your heels. Move your head back and rest it on the back of your neck. Keep your eyes looking upwards for a few moments while continuing to breathe deeply. Repeat about three times.

3rd Eye Mudra Exercise: You may have seen hands and fingers take an interesting shape or form during yoga practice or meditation. The various positions and connecting of the thumb and fingers are sacred gestures *called 'mudras',* and like all other practices in yoga, they have purpose and significance. Mudras function as a unifying force to bring together and balance the body through the hands. A mudra is a gesture or seal used in yoga. The practice of these gestures and seals channel the flow of prana life force. Ayurveda explains the body as being made up of five elements; fire, air, space, earth and water. A healthy body has a balance of these elements. Conversely, a dominating or weakening element would cause an imbalance in the body and have a negative impact on one's health. This would manifest as illness or disease. There are five elements and five fingers. Each finger represents an according element. In yoga philosophy, it is said that through each finger, runs the prana for each element. By manipulating the pranas we can increase or decrease the prana to a specific part of the body. That is why a mudra is also referred to as a seal. We are sealing or locking the pranas for a specific purpose. When a specific mudra is used for a specific purpose, it can help restore the balance of the five elements of the body using prana. The fingers represent, accordingly, each element: the Thumb represents the fire element; the Index finger represents the air element; the Middle finger represents the space element; the Ring finger represents the earth element and the Pinky finger represents the water element. As we have two hands, so do we have two sides of the body; solar energy on the right side and lunar energy on the left side. The Mudras work to singularly stimulate solar or lunar energy. And part from balancing energies in the body, mudras are also used in meditation and yoga practice to enhance focus and help direct our awareness inwards. There are many mudras for meditation and yoga, each with its own unique purpose and benefit for the mind, body and spirit. One of the most simple is to sit on the floor with your legs crossed and your back straight. Place your palms together in front of you with both thumbs touching and tilted towards your chest. Both of your middle fingers should be touching as well. The rest of your fingers should be bent. Inhale deeply through your nose, and as you exhale, utter the mantra

'**Ksham**' while focusing on your brow chakra. Repeat seven times.

- **3rd Eye Mantra:** The word '**OM**' is often chanted like a mantra in spiritual practices because it actually matches the vibration of the 3rd Eye. It creates healing energy that balances and nurtures the 3rd Eye Chakra. Lie or sit comfortably and focus on your 3rd Eye. Chant the word '**OM**' in a monotone voice over and over. Feel the vibrations of the mantra flowing into your 3rd Eye and visualise it vibrating along with the mantra. Practise for as long as you wish.

So there you have it!   All you have to do now is get practising!

Chapter 7:

What to expect

Activating your 3rd Eye will enrich and transform your life! And why? Simply because you have now begun a process of metamorphosis! You are now looking at all aspects of life through a different lens! And you can never go back to how you were seeing things before! This is a one-way street you are now on! One direction only! That means no u-turns! And anyone and everyone can do it! Awakening your 3rd Eye does not belong to any particular religion or creed, - this is a spiritual experience, - religion and spirituality being two very different things! And to repeat! - This is for everyone!

Awakening your 3rd Eye is not some mystical, abstract concept! Awakening your 3rd Eye is simply activating a vital and necessary centre of energy within your body that has lain dormant within you for an unknown number of years. Awakening your 3rd Eye is **not** about accessing knowledge gained from experience and learning in this physical world, - but an awakening of one's insight, intuition and psychic abilities, - enabling you to access levels of insight, awareness and other realms of consciousness above and beyond your very limited two-eye vision and your very limited five physical senses. Awareness of other dimensions in the entirety of creation, only when looking through the lens of the 3rd Eye and the wealth of wisdom that is available therein is what ancient spiritual traditions discovered and which countless peoples across the world continue to experience and enjoy today.

As your 3rd eye chakra begins to open with the exercises, you will begin to experience a gradual change. It may be almost imperceptible at first, but you will feel it. Don't expect too much early on, however. Give yourself time, stay open, and be patient. After all, your 3rd eye has been dormant all your life. It needs time to open and slowly come to life. You can expect to experience some of the following:

- A slight headache or pressure in the area of the 3rd Eye chakra, especially when you wake up in the morning. The pressure may be quite strong as if something is pressing down on your brow, or it could be slight. This is a sign that your 3rd eye is expanding

- A tingling sensation in the 3rd Eye area

- You may hear slight popping sounds in your head at various intervals during the day

- You may experience increased sensitivity to bright or artificial light

- Your physical senses will be heightened, where you will see, hear, feel, taste and smell with a new level of awareness

- Your self-worth value and self-esteem will be increased, simply because you will see that your previous feelings of self-doubt and lack of confidence have come from societal standards, to which you now no longer adhere

- As your 3rd Eye becomes activated, it will be more perceptive of toxins and additives in food. So you will become more health-conscious! In fact, your diet might change completely!

- You will notice an improvement in your concentration and focus

- You will experience increased and improved memory

- The 3rd Eye casts light on truth. And once a light is turned on in any dark room, everything can be seen in perspective. So too, when you open your 3rd Eye, you cast more light on new knowledge and grasp its meaning much more easily

- You will be less biased in your decision making, as you will '*see*' the various perspectives much more clearly. And seeing all the pieces of the puzzle allows you to see the most effective solution

- You will be more aware of the energy around other people and how you are affected by them

- You may sense that something is going to happen before it actually occurs. For example, you might think about someone, and then they appear unexpectedly at your door, or you meet them in the street. Or you might '***see***' some event happening before it becomes common knowledge

The above are just some of the physical manifestations of your 3rd Eye opening and being activated. But more significant is how the activation of your 3rd Eye will contribute to how you '**see**' life and what is going on all around us in the world at this time. Your 3rd Eye will enable you and guide you to stay positive in this increasingly negative, hostile, aggressive and war-torn world.

While others see doom and gloom all around, your 3rd Eye will keep you positive! And this despite all the dire predictions for 2024 and beyond!

So what do you '**see**' through the lens of your 3rd Eye that others do not see? Others who are looking only through their two physical eyes? Others who are listening to the news in mainstream media?

They see and hear only all those dire predictions! All that deliberate scare-mongering! All those depressing and grim headlines! And those depressing and grim headlines are causing people to feel fear, despair, anger and a sense of complete and utter helplessness and hopelessness, - believing we are facing the end of the world! Some are freaking out, in total melt-down, turning to alcohol, drugs and other artificial stimulants to get them through. Either this or they are totally unaware of what is going on, or choosing to ignore it all in the hope that it will somehow all disappear.

And you who are looking through the lens of your 3rd Eye? How are you **'seeing'** it all?

You are not giving into fear, anger or despair. And why not? Because you **'know'** that yes, the world is indeed ending, but not as many others envision this. The world **as we know it** is dying. But it is not the end of humanity.

You **'know'** that endings must precede new beginnings! And endings can be so beautiful! Like the trees shedding their leaves in the kaleidoscopic splendour and extravaganza of colour that we call Autumn.

You **'know'** that the old 3rd dimensional energy of our Planet Earth is giving way to a much higher level of consciousness, a greater level of awareness.

You **'know'** that more and more people are waking up like never before to the corruption in all areas of life, - in our governments, in our financial institutions, in our controlling religions, in our education systems, etc.

You **'know'** that it is the big armaments and weapons manufacturers and the big pharmaceutical and drug companies who are ruling this world and keeping us in war and ill health, - that small elite that controls governments and world leaders.

You '*see*' through all the lies, all the deceptions, all the distortions of the truth, all the scams, all the gameplaying, controlling mechanisms that have been used to keep humanity in a servile position and condition.

You '*see*' how all the diversities and differences in our world are being deliberately exploited and fostered in order to distract us from what is really going on.

You '*see*' that out of all of this, a new earth is being born. Our planet is in the process of ascending into the higher 5th dimension energy frequency level. The level of unconditional love!

You '*see*' that this is the time for which we agreed to be here, - to help raise the spiritual consciousness of all humanity.

You '*see*' the great spiritual awakening going on all around us right now, a spiritual awakening not just on a personal level, but also the awakening to an awareness of ourselves as multidimensional beings and an inherent part of the great Cosmic Energy, of All THAT IS.

You '*see*' humanity beginning to experience this new higher frequency consciousness, and you '*know*' that 2024 will continue to bring enormous changes and endings on many levels.

You *'know'* that all is well, that our earth is experiencing normal disturbances and changes as we ascend into and take our rightful place amongst the higher vibration levels of the cosmos. Everything happens in cycles, and we are currently in a cycle of great change, reformation and renewal.

So what are you waiting for? -   Bring it on!

EPILOGUE

As we have seen throughout this book, our 3rd Eye is also our 6th Chakra, and most importantly, our FIRST sense, and not our sixth, as we have often been led to believe. It is our centre of intuition, inner knowing, inner wisdom, psychic powers, - literally seeing beyond what we see with our two physical eyes. - Vision beyond physical sight!

Our two eyes are not all-seeing! They allow us to see only 5% of what is there. And what is there is the illusion, not the reality. We are conditioned, programmed to see only what we are being allowed to see, - that's the illusion!

The difference in seeing with our two eyes only and seeing with our 3rd Eye can be described as standing up close to a brick wall where we see only the brick right in front of us. But when we take a step back, move back away from the wall, we see the entire wall, and then as we move further back again we see the entire building, then the entire street, and so on. Or like the tiny insect on the ground and the eagle in the air. The little insect on the ground is very limited in its vision, unlike the eagle that sees everything from its higher vantage point. Or like the little grub in the murky pond! How different and expansive its view of life becomes when it manages to break the surface and transmute into a dragon fly, spreading its wings and flying off.

So we need to activate our 3rd Eye! And why? Simply because activating our 3rd Eye is the key to the survival of humanity as a species! And it is the **only** way! Not having it activated, and therefore seeing only with our two physical eyes, - this is what is keeping us locked and trapped in this 3rd dimension energy vibration frequency level. Humanity is on a very slippery slope right now, a landslide even, on the cliff edge, - whatever way you want to describe it! And our future as a species? A future of AI, war, threat of nuclear war, famine, destitution etc?

And the answer? We need to get onto the 5th dimension energy vibration level! The energy vibration of unconditional love! To where the negative, stagnant energies that are controlling and running rampant in our world cannot gain access! - And why not? Because we EARN access to higher dimensions, by raising our consciousness, our awareness, and these negative energies cannot access 5th dimension energy level because they know nothing of love. So by getting ourselves onto the 5th dimension, - the dimension of unconditional love, - we are out of their reach! They just cannot get to us!

In the 5th dimension there is no judgement, no criticism, but just total acceptance of all diversities and differences. And this does not mean that we see only the good in other people. Seeing only the good in other people is like being in denial. Of course no one is perfect! But being on the 5th energy vibration frequency means that we **'see'** beyond this, - with our 3rd Eye!

And how do we get onto the 5th dimension? - By activating our 3rd eye and keeping it healthy. This is the key! The only way humanity can survive any longer as a species is by activating our 3rd Eye, raising our consciousness level! Because the trap we are caught in is a **consciousness** trap!

Evolution is not just a physical thing. It is spiritual, - raising our **consciousness,** to get above this war-torn, decimated world! Getting out of this quagmire! We are caught in a **consciousness** trap! Caught because we are seeing with only our two physical eyes!

The problems of our world are neither political nor

economic. They are spiritual! So we must seek and apply a spiritual solution! We have got to change our viewing, - like the way you adjust the lens of a camera! To get the proper clear focus! Change our mind-set! And for that we need to work through our 3rd Eye! But how can we if it is shut? If we are not activating it? We cannot solve war with more war! An eye for an eye and a tooth for a tooth! We all end up blind and toothless! - Charming!

And mainstream media! Mainstream media make us all believe that all this violence, hatred, war, etc is normal! But it is not normal! This is not our world! The majority of humanity are loving, kind, caring, but we never see that side on the media! We are seeing only with our 2two physical eyes! We are seeing only what **they** want us to see! We need to activate our 3rd Eye! Using only our two eyes, - this is what is keeping us trapped in this dense, lower vibration level we call earth! So we need to stop listening to the media! Turn it off! Close your ears! Do not get caught up in all this drama and gameplaying! And do not try to fight back! Because in fighting back we become like them! By giving them attention, we are strengthening them! So IGNORE IT ALL! LET IT ALL GO! USE YOUR 3rd EYE!

When you wake up in the morning, your eyes open and

you see the world around you! BUT! This GREAT
AWAKENING that is taking right place now! It is the 3rd
Eye that is awakening, opening! A spiritual awakening!
And more and more psychic children are coming in
now, - star, rainbow, crystal, - who all seem to have
their 3rd Eye open, and their two physical eyes
somewhat dimmed! As a result, these children are
much more alert, much more aware!

Opening your 3rd Eye! That is what this book has been
all about! So, for the sake of the future of humanity,
start practising now! And you know what practice does!
- Practice makes perfect! And practice combined with
patience? - Well, that's surely an unbeatable
combination!

Other Books by Eileen McCourt

Eileen has written 47 other books, including her first audio-book. All are available on Amazon. For more information, visit her author page:

www.tinyurl.com/EileenMcCourt

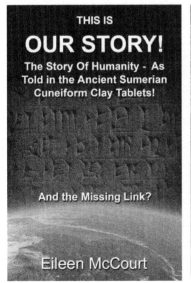

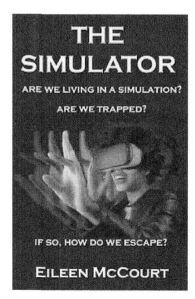

Other books by Eileen McCourt

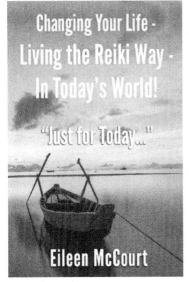

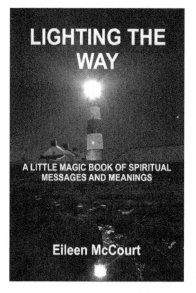

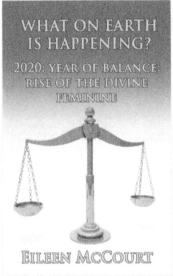

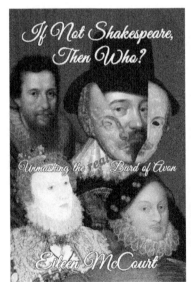

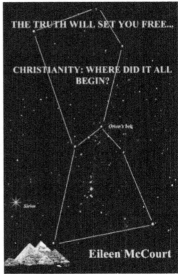

Audiobook

Other books by Eileen McCourt

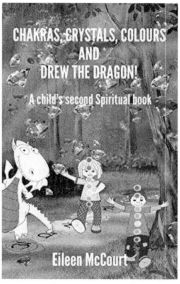

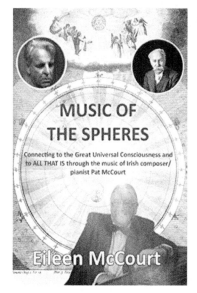

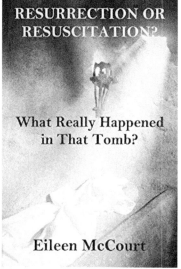

Other books by Eileen McCourt

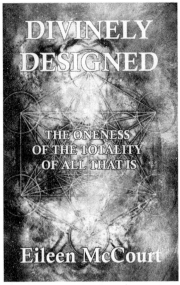

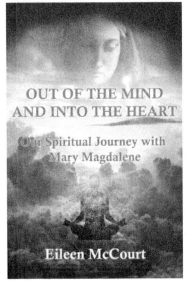

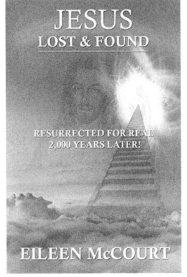

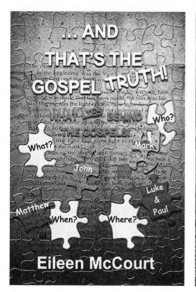

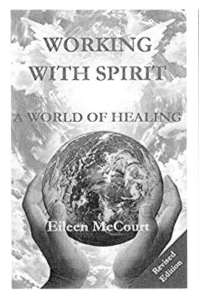

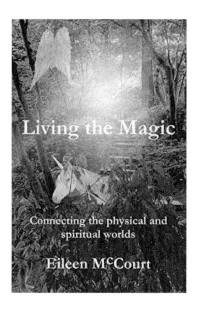

Printed in Great Britain
by Amazon

43167726R00066